# OPERATIONS SECURITY - OPSEC

## WHAT IS OPSEC?

OPSEC, short for Operations Security, is a tool to deny adversaries the Critical Information or 'CI' they require to harm you, your family, your organization or our national security.

The reasons for practicing OPSEC are:

1. Protect you and your family against:
   - Criminal threats
   - Foreign threats while traveling
   - Threats to your livelihood

2. Protect your organization against:
   - Economic competitors
   - Foreign espionage
   - Criminal threats
   - Terrorism

3. Protect our nation against:
   - Economic espionage
   - Military espionage
   - Terrorism

In order to practice OPSEC, you must understand who your adversaries are, identify the CI they seek and take measures to prevent the release of that CI.

## UNDERSTANDING YOUR ADVERSARIES

The range of adversaries and their objectives:

- Burglars - theft of valuable goods
- Robbers - theft of money or valuable goods
- Terrorists - fear, intimidation, economic damage

**UNDERSTANDING YOUR ADVERSARIES** (continued)

- Kidnappers - ransom, intimidation
- Extremists - intimidation, public awareness of their cause
- Revenge Motivated Individuals - intimidation, revenge
- Economic Competitors - theft of trade secrets, knowhow
- Foreign Intelligence Agents - military capabilities, government intent

Adversary targets:

- Burglars: Homes, vehicles, offices, hotel rooms
- Robbers: Travelers, individuals in secluded or dark areas
- Terrorists: Critical manufacturing and infrastructure, public places, tourist locations,  transportation nodes, military or government facilities
- Kidnappers: Executives and their family members, travelers
- Extremists: Executives and their property, facility critical infrastructure, operations corporate events
- Revenge Motivated Individuals: Executives, managers and co-workers, company infrastructure
- Economic Competitors: Strategic plans, sales and financial data, trade secrets
- Foreign Intelligence Agents: Military deployment plans, military equipment specifications, diplomatic communiques

## WHAT IS CRITICAL INFORMATION (CI)?

CI is the information that adversaries seek in order to carry out their plans. We must prevent our adversaries from accessing CI.

Adversaries' objectives and targets determine what CI they need. For example:

Terrorists planning to attack a public-use facility require CI on:

- Security camera coverage
- Security guard and police presence
- Access points
- Facility layouts showing non-public areas

If you were responsible for protecting this facility, you would need to take steps to prevent the release of the CI.

Now consider the CI that *your* adversaries are seeking about you, your movements and your work. Look at your life through the eyes of your adversaries and ask yourself questions such as:

What time do you leave for work? What route do you take? Is your house empty when you leave? What sensitive information do you possess about your  organization? Where do you keep it? How is it protected? Is unique equipment used for product testing? Is the equipment visible from the  outside? What is your travel itinerary? Who are you meeting? Why are you meeting?

The answers to these questions provide the CI your adversaries require. This is what must be protected.

## OPSEC INDICATORS

Indicators are observable behaviors or physical features that are harmless when considered independently; however, when combined with other indicators, they identify exploitable security vulnerabilities or provide an adversary with CI.

For example, imagine you are on vacation and you forgot to cancel your newspaper subscription. Over the days, the newspapers will pile up in front of your door. The indicator is the newspaper pile and the CI is 'nobody is home'! Below are other examples of indicators, and CI:

**An unusually large lunch order is placed at the office:**

This is an indicator. The lunch order is a change to the usual pattern of food ordering, suggesting a large gathering or event at the office.

**An providing the names of visitors to a secure facility with the time and date for a future meeting:**

This is CI. The information tells an adversary when, where and who is coming to the facility.

**A rectangular saw cut shape is visible in the pavement inside and outside a vehicle entrance gate:**

This is an indicator. The rectangular shape indicates magnetic loop induction which automatically opens the gate when a vehicle approaches.

**A design drawing for a prototype of a new military vehicle.:**

This is CI. The information provides the adversary with the vehicle dimensions and engineering specifications. An adversary can use this information to help their country build and sell a similar vehicle (economic competition) or to defeat the new vehicle on the battlefield.

## INDICATOR QUICK REFERENCE

Indicators of Organizational Control and Structure:

- Organizational chart
- Website 'About Us' information
- Personnel contact list
- Organizational policies
- Job-related information on Linkedin, Spoke, Plaxo, etc.

Indicators of Communications/Telecommunications Usage:

- New wireless network names (SSIDs)
- Wireless network names that correlate to an activity
- Sudden increase or decrease in radio traffic
- Use of call signs that correlate to an activity

Indicators of Research and Testing:

- Presence of public media, writers for technical journals
- Budget data for R&D
- Presence of specialized equipment for testing
- Presence of video cameras for testing
- Special security zones and restrictions before/during test

Indicators of Operational Activity:

- Scope of work orders
- Capabilities and specialization of newly hired personnel
- Meeting notes
- Operating plans
- Employee suggestions
- Work schedules

Indicators of Personal and Work-Related Movement:

- Public tracking of aircraft FAA tail numbers
- Personal and work mail
- Driving routes

**INDICATOR QUICK REFERENCE** (continued)

- Geotag information contained in photos
- Images posted to the Web

**CI QUICK REFERENCE**

CI regarding Facility Security:

- Guard/police presence
- Guard patrol zones/frequency/procedures
- Automatic vehicle detection for gate operation
- Property illumination and dark spots
- Security camera coverage
- Personnel operation of secure access doors
- Procedures for display of ID

CI regarding Operations:

- Operational tactics, techniques and procedures
- Movement and schedules of key personnel
- Peak facility utilization times
- Strategic sales plans
- Government contract information
- Organizational partnerships and agreements
- Design plans, trade secrets and intellectual property

# OPEN SOURCE INFORMATION

The modern adversary has access to an incredible range of tools for the collection of CI. These tools include social media sites, data aggregation sites, powerful search tools, public and private imagery resources and proven human collection techniques.

As information collection capabilities expand, individuals and organizations are increasingly vulnerable to the tactics of their adversaries unless they practice OPSEC to protect their CI.

A key step in protecting CI is the Critical Information List (CIL), which is simply a list of the information that your range of adversaries require to carry out their plans. The CIL allows you to recognize your CI and take steps to protect it.

## WHAT IS OPEN SOURCE INFORMATION?

Open source information is information that is publicly or openly accessible. Adversaries use it to collect CI which yields actionable intelligence (OSINT) when context is applied.

Some sources of Open Source Information:

- Company website
- Published technical journals
- Printed, television, radio and online news sources
- Web-based social media information
- Electronic documents accessible via the Web

Common Information Collection Tools:

- Web search engines (Google, Bing, Yahoo, Duck Duck Go)
- Web crawlers (Screaming Frog, Apify, Deep Crawl)
- Social Media (Twitter, Linkedin, Facebook, Instagram)
- Published technical journals

## WHAT IS OPEN SOURCE INFORMATION? (continued)

Common Information Collection Tools (continued):

- Visualization tools (Maltego, SiloBreaker, i2 Analyst)
- Dark Web (Tor Browser, DarkOwl, ThomasNet)
- News (CNN, Google News, Al-Jazeera, ITAR-TASS)
- Imagery (Google Earth, USGS Earth Explorer, Bing Maps)
- Other Specialized Tools
    - FOCA (Extracts Metadata from Web documents)
    - Google Hacks (Google search terms to hack systems)
    - Whois (Website ownership and administration info)
    - Wayback Machine (accesses old archived web pages)
    - EXIF Viewer (reads geotagged photo information)

## OSINT COLLECTION COUNTERMEASURES

- *Develop a Critical Information List (CIL)*
- Review website information against CIL
- Review product and marketing material against CIL
- Do not post your personal or family details in social media
- Review Linkedin and other social media sites against CIL
- Do not geotag and post work related images to Web
- Do not mention plans, intentions or activities to the Press
- Conduct random Web searches for personal or work CI
- Do not mention trips, projects or work in social media
- Disable public tracking of corporate aircraft tail number

# OBSERVATION-BASED INFORMATION

## WHAT IS OBSERVATION-BASED INFORMATION?

Observation-based OPSEC vulnerabilities refers to the human collection of information through observation. Observation may be conducted with plain eyesight, through an optical device such as binoculars, or through auditory observation (listening to someone's conversation).

Adversaries use observation to learn behaviors and operating patterns. Their tactics might be covert or overt.

Covert (hidden) observation may be conducted out of your sight (concealment) or in plain view, but carried out under the pretext of some legitimate activity (a cover).

## TYPES OF OBSERVATION

Examples of observation under concealment:

- Camouflaged and watching from the bushes
- Peeking out of a parked car
- Watching from the window of an adjacent building

Examples of observation under a cover:

- Watching your facility operations while sitting at bus stop
- Observing your movements while pushing a baby stroller
- Sitting in a coffee shop listening to your work conversation
- Dressed like a construction worker to loiter outside your facility and take notes on its activities

## POTENTIAL OBSERVATION TARGETS

- Security guard patrol zones
- Security cameras and field of vision
- Facility perimeter defenses

## POTENTIAL OBSERVATION TARGETS (continued

- Visible physical security vulnerabilities
- Parking spots of key personnel
- Personnel use of access cards and secure doors
- Facility ID badges
- Work-related documents
- Your home security features
- Your home for indicators that it is unoccupied

## OBSERVATION COUNTERMEASURES

- *Review your CIL*
- Randomized security guard patrol zones and patrol times
- Install perimeter fence mesh to reduce facility observation
- Employees should not misuse security procedures
- Do not display ID badge when outside facility property
- Never hold work-related conversations in public place
- Use project code names in work discussions/documents
- Never leave work documents, data devices, etc. in vehicle
- Avoid bringing work documents home
- Micro cross-shred personal/work information for disposal
- Remove indicators that your home is unoccupied
    - Cancel your newspaper and have mail collected
    - Use automatic light timers

## WHAT IS WEB-BASED INFORMATION?

The Internet is an enormous system of inter-connected networks that hosts governmental, educational, commercial and private computers.

The World Wide Web (the Web) is an information access and sharing system that we all use all the time. It provides access to Internet computer content via web pages, e-mail systems, file directories, and computer applications.

The Web has changed the way we all live our lives and conduct our work and will continue to impact us in the years ahead. It has also provided a target rich environment for our adversaries to exploit how we use Web-based information.

## ADVERSARIAL USE OF THE WEB

The following adversaries are exploiting our use of the Web:

- Criminals
- Business competitors
- Foreign intelligence agents
- Terrorists
- Stalkers
- Hackers
- Pedophiles
- Identity thieves
- Identity brokers

Each adversary will use the Web to exploit other users (you) and gain access to CI and indicators. How they exploit your use of the Web depends more on the opportunities you provide to them and less on their sophistication.

## ADVERSARIAL USE OF THE WEB (continued)

Each adversary will use the Web to exploit other users (you) and gain access to CI and indicators. How they exploit your use of the Web depends more on the opportunities you provide to them and less on their sophistication.

The following are examples of Web vulnerabilities that provide CI and indicators:

- Blog discussions where technical information is divulged
- Posting capabilities and qualifications in personal profiles
- Posting technical and professional affiliations
- Supplier or purchasing data files accessible by Web server
- Images on social media indicating event locations
- Images on social media showing your home or location
- Images showing geodata
- Future movements and actions posted in social media
- Phishing scams (fraudulent e-mails to steal personal info)
- Trojan horse and computer virus infection

## WEB-BASED COUNTERMEASURES

- _Review your CIL_
- Review company website against CIL
- Do not post or discuss project technical details online
- Do not show professional affiliations or qualifications
- Create CIL with suppliers/contractors for their use
- Review images for background indicators or geotags
- Do not post any information on future intent/movements
- Do not click hyperlinks from unknown/unusual e-mails

## WHAT IS IMAGERY INTELLIGENCE?

Imagery intelligence (IMINT) is the analysis of images to detect, identify and classify objects. IMINT can provide an adversary with excellent understanding of a location's layout, utilization and usage patterns. It can also provide valuable indicators of operational procedures.

## IMAGERY SOURCES

There are various free and commercial  online imagery services available to the public. These services include satellite images, aerial images taken from aircraft or photographs taken from individuals. Free imagery typically provide recent images with good quality for detailed observation of facility layout, design features and identification of objects.

The following are some free imagery sources:

- Google Earth and Google Images
- Bing Images
- Yahoo Images
- Flash Earth
- Terrafly
- National Geographic MapMachine

Fee-based commercial imagery provide near real-time, higher quality images than free services, and can provide an adversary with details on object size, shape, use, etc.

The following are some paid imagery sources:

- GeoEye
- Digital Globe
- L3Harris Geospatial
- Spire Global

## IMAGERY SOURCES (continued)

It is also important to note that foreign intelligence services from certain countries will possess imagery capabilities that exceed the best commercially available quality. These may be directed at U.S. organizations to carry out economic or military espionage.

## IMAGERY TARGETS

- Location or movement of critical infrastructure
- Identification of object size, shape, markings
- Facility design features, roof hatches, roof ladders, etc.
- Changes to normal operating patterns, e.g. vehicle types

## IMAGERY-BASED COUNTERMEASURES

- *Review your CIL*
- Do not bring sensitive objects outside until needed
- Keep sensitive objects under tarp
- Make covered objects appear larger to confuse adversary
- Randomize timing of outdoor testing, equipment use
- Cover equipment markings
- Note N-Number of suspicious aircraft over facility location
- Randomize timing of outdoor testing, equipment use

# COMMUNICATIONS INTELLIGENCE

## WHAT IS COMMUNICATIONS INTELLIGENCE?

Our adversaries possess the capability to intercept personal and work communications. Their actions may range from the interception of transmissions to access of discarded equipment containing CI to the physical theft of equipment. The hostile acquisition of our communications is referred to as Communications Intelligence (COMINT).

## COMMUNICATIONS SECURITY (COMSEC)

Communications Security (COMSEC) is a wide ranging field that includes many disciplines of electronic communications. It deals with the security of our person-to-person transmissions.

For our purposes we will consider COMSEC to address the following:

- Wireless computer networks
- E-mail
- Radio transmissions
- Telephone transmissions
- Cell phone transmissions and data storage
- Fascimile (Fax) transmissions and data storage
- Networked printer hub stations (print/fax/scan/e-mail)
- File transfer applications (Skype, Messenger, IM, etc.)
- Computer storage devices (not really COMSEC but critical)

## COMSEC THREATS

Your adversaries will possess a range of capabilities by which they can target your communications and gather COMINT:

## COMSEC THREATS

- Business competitors may employ personnel with intelligence gathering backgrounds, using highly sophisticated techniques

- Terrorists may use proven techniques learned in combat environments and may be trained by foreign experts

- Foreign intelligence agents backed by their State's assets may use powerful tools and techniques to target your organization's strategic plans and technical secrets

The following are some of the actions that your adversaries might take to target your COMSEC:

- Infecting a personal or work computer to conduct network surveillance on transmitted data to acquire usernames and passwords

- Searching for wireless network SSID to identify a network dedicated to a specific operation or purpose

- Tapping telephone lines to eavesdrop on conversations

- Cracking WEP enabled  or unprotected wireless networks to browse files

- Radio frequency scanners to eavesdrop on unencrypted conversations

- Tapping telephone lines to eavesdrop on conversations

- Cell phone scanners to eavesdrop on conversations

- Bluetooth hacking of cell phones and computers to steal contacts and data

- Conduct a Man-in-the-Middle attack to intercept your smartphone incoming mobile data and transmit to the intended recipient, allowing undetected data monitoring

- Access your discarded optical fax rolls which can be unrolled to read imprinted text from previous fax printouts

# COMMUNICATIONS INTELLIGENCE (continued)

## COMSEC THREATS (continued)

- Posing as an office cleaner, supplier or copier technician to access networked printer hubs and print out e-mail, scanned and sent/received fax information from the memory buffer

- Theft of laptop computers and portable storage devices

## COMSEC VULNERABILITIES

- Sending unencrypted e-mails containing passwords and sensitive information

- Using open or WEP enabled wireless computer networks

- Wireless network SSIDs that correlate to an operation

- Using unencrypted radios for sensitive operations

- Failing to use code words while using unencrypted radios

- Sensitive discussions on unencrypted landline telephone

- Discussing sensitive information on a cell phone

- Using an unencrypted Bluetooth link

- Sending sensitive information via cell phone SMS, instant messenger services or file transfer

- Sending sensitive information via unencrypted fax

- Failing to destroy thermal fax ribbons before discarding

- Networked printer hub stations that retain the information in their memory buffer

- Using a public file transfer service to transfer sensitive files over the Web

- Failing to secure laptop computers and portable storage devices when out of your possession to prevent their theft

These are common vulnerabilities that adversaries exploit to intercept and steal sensitive and damaging information in your personal and work-related communications.

## COMSEC COUNTERMEASURES

- Ensure that your computer has active virus protection with updated virus definitions
- Use WPA2 encryption on your wireless computer network
- Do not e-mail, SMS or IM sensitive information from phone
- Password protect your phone and use approved third party encryption to protect data if phone is lost or stolen
- Use e-mail encryption to send sensitive e-mails
- Use approved full disk encryption on your computer or portable storage devices to protect data if lost or stolen
- Do not hold sensitive conversations on unencrypted radios, or landline telephones
- Have your landline utility box moved inside your house
- Incinerate thermal fax ribbons prior to discarding
- Set networked printer hubs to clear memory buffer after each use

## WHAT IS TRASH INTELLIGENCE?

Trash Intelligence (TRASHINT) refers to the CI contained in discarded materials and accessed by adversaries to carry out their objectives. Scouring through garbage, popularly known as 'dumpster diving' is a highly effective means of accessing CI.

Many organization have policies requiring the shredding of sensitive information, but have no procedures for personnel to identify and protect CI - thus CI gets discarded in the trash. Likewise, personal trash can also contain valuable CI to your adversaries.

Note: Dumpster diving may not be ethical, but its practice as a criminal or legal matter is open to State by State interpretation. At present, misdemeanor charges such as trespassing are the most likely consequence and therefore not a deterrent to your adversaries.

## TRASHINT VULNERABILITIES

The following are common vulnerabilities that can be exploited by your adversaries to gain TRASHINT:

- Organization has not created a CIL
- No procedures for identifying CI prior to discarding trash
- No internal audit of trash to ensure no CI is discarded
- Trash and recyclable bins are unsecured

## COMMONLY DISCARDED CI

The following are examples of types of CI commonly discarded in the trash:

- Organizational contact lists
- Internal memos, printed e-mails, inter-office communiques
- Courier shipping receipts and waybills
- Purchasing information
- Training materials
- Strategic organizational documents, plans
- Hiring data and other Human Resources data
- Upcoming travel reservations or itinerary information
- Bills and payment stubs
- Operating manuals and user guides
- Schedules or shift staffing data
- Network addresses, IP configurations or IT configurations
- Banking statements or financial or credit card statements

## TRASHINT COLLECTION COUNTERMEASURES

- *Review your CIL*
- Conduct periodic internal dumpster dives against the CIL
- Conduct reviews of recycling bin contents against the CIL
- Shred documents containing indicators and CI with a micro cross-shredder
- If you use a shred bin, lock the bin to prevent content removal
- Place shed bins in secure areas
- Place trash, recycling and shred bins in secure area with proper lighting and monitoring
- Electronic storage media must be adequately degaussed (wiped) before discarding, e.g. CD/DVD, magnetic tape, hard drives

# SOCIAL ENGINEERING & ELICITATION

## WHAT IS SOCIAL ENGINEERING?

Social engineering is the art of manipulating people to make them believe you are someone you are not in order to gain access to protected information or secured areas. Social engineering can be used by adversaries to gain CI to plan for a range of hostile acts including: cyber attack, to gain movement intelligence on a targeted person(s), to deceive personnel and security into granting access to a secure location or secured information, etc.

## WHAT IS ELICITATION?

Elicitation is a technique used to discreetly gather information from an unsuspecting person by a face to face conversation, over the phone or by written message. When conducted by a skilled adversary, the elicitation will appear to be a normal social or professional conversation.

## TACTICS AND TECHNIQUES

The following are some examples of tactics and techniques your adversaries might use to socially engineer access or elicit information:

- An adversary calls a company posing as technical support and asks to be connected with his intended target. Once connected, the adversary advises his target that he is improving security on the target's computer and asks for their username, password,  description of the file directory structure, etc.

- An adversary approaches the guard post at an entrance to a secure facility and asks the guard if the company is hiring workers. This allows the adversary to see inside the guard shack and determine whether guards are armed and if they monitor security camera feeds on the property.

## TACTICS AND TECHNIQUES (continued)

- An adversary posing as a tourist approaches an employee outside of a company and engages in conversation about the city. Eventually, the conversation focuses on the company, what it does, what kind of products they make, why they are a good stock pick, etc.

- An adversary posing as a fellow business traveler starts a conversation with their target in a bar. The adversary uses seemingly innocent questions to ask about the target's line of work, their internal operations, and reason for the business  trip.

## SOCIAL ENGINEERING & ELICITATION COUNTER-MEASURES

A proven defense against social engineering and elicitation is awareness of the threat and their tactics. Awareness training and self-education (there are many resources on the Web) will help you to recognize suspicious behaviors and potential attempts by adversaries at eliciting information or trying to socially engineer unauthorized access. Implementing a company 'enquiry response procedure' with prepared answers is also effective to help personnel avoid targeting and exploitation.

Some basic rules for becoming a hard target are:

- Do not allow observation of work related documents while in public places

- If approached by a stranger, be aware of potential elicitation

- Do not provide any details about your work or private life -if asked, politely change the subject

- If approached by someone asking for access to a secure site or protected information, always ask them to provide official identification and a phone number to verify their identity

# GLOSSARY OF TERMS

**Critical Information (CI)** - Information that adversaries seek in order to carry out their plans.

**Critical Information  List (CIL)** - A list of the information you possess that your adversaries require to carry out their plans

**Elicitation** -  A technique used to discreetly gather information from an unsuspecting person

**Full Disk Encryption** - Encryption of all data on a device

**Geotags** - Geographical information added to various media

**Indicators** - Observable behaviors or physical features that provide CI when combined with other indicators

**Man-in-the-Middle Attack** - A method of eavesdropping on electronic messages between two or more parties

**Operations Security (OPSEC)** - A tool to deny CI to adversaries

**Service Set Identification (SSID)** - A wireless network identifier

**Social Engineering** -Manipulation through deception to gain access to protected information or secured areas.

**Thermal Fax Ribbon** - An ink ribbon used by thermal fax machines that retains information transferred to paper

**Wireless Equivalent Privacy (WEP)** - An exploitable method of wireless encryption

**Wireless Protected Access (WPA2)** - A method of encryption for wireless networks providing more protection than WEP

# ACRONYMS

**CI** - Critical Information

**CIL** - Critical Information List

**COMINT** - Communications Intelligence

**COMSEC** - Communications Security

**DVR** - Digital Video Recorder

**FAA** - Federal Aviation Authority

**IM** - Instant Messenger

**IMINT** - Imagery Intelligence

**OPSEC** - Operations Security

**OSINT** - Open Source Intelligence

**SMS** - Short Message Service

**SSID** - Service Set Identification

**TRASHINT** - Trash Intelligence

**WEP** - Wireless Equivalent Privacy

**WPA2** - Wireless Protected Access